1527	Estevanico leads exploration of New Mexico and Arizona
1619	First African slaves brought to North America
1670	Slavery legalised in America
1777	Vermont becomes the first state to abolish slavery
1808	African slave-trade banned in America
1865	Thirteenth Amendment to the Constitution, abolishing slavery
1866	Ku Klux Klan founded
1870	Fifteenth Amendment, banning voting discrimination
1877	Federal troops withdraw from the South
1881	Tennessee becomes the first state to pass a Jim Crow law
1908	National Association for the Advancement of Coloured People (NAACP) founded
1917	United States enters First World War to "make the world safe for democracy."
1919	Twenty-six race riots take place in the United States
1920	Marcus Garvey forms Universal Improvement Association
1927	Marcus Garvey deported from the United States
1935	National Council of Negro Women founded
	Congress refuses to pass Anti-Lynching legislation
1936	Jessie Owens wins four gold medals in Berlin Olympics
1941	Racial discrimination in armaments industry prohibited
1944	Congress of Racial Equality (CORE) formed
1946	Segregated inter-state bus travel banned by Supreme Court
	Truman sets up Committee on Civil Rights
1948	Discrimination in the armed forces banned
1952	First year without a lynching since 1881
1954	Supreme Court rules that segregation in schools is unconstitutional
	Benjamin Davis, becomes the first black general in United States Air-Force
	Montgomery bus boycott begins
	Last all-black units in the armed forces disbanded
1957	Dr. Martin Luther King becomes President of Southern Christian Leadership Conference
	Federal troops sent to Little Rock, Arkansas
1960	First student sit-in against segregation at lunch-counters
	Student Nonviolent Coordinating Committee (SNCC) formed
	Elijah Muhammad calls for the creation of a separate state for blacks

1961	Freedom riders in the South arrested
1963	Federal troops sent to ensure James Meredith can attend Mississippi University
	Medgar Evers, NAACP leader assassinated
	250,000 civil rights demonstrators march on Washington
	Birmingham church bombing kills four black children
1964	Riots in Harlem, Jersey City, Philadelphia, Rochester and Chicago
	Civil Rights Bill passed by Congress
	Martin Luther King wins Nobel Peace Prize
1965	Malcolm X assassinated
	Dr. Martin Luther King leads large march from Selma to Montgomery
	Voting Rights Bill passed
	Thirty-four people killed in riots in Watts, Los Angeles
1966	Stokely Carmichael introduces the idea of 'Black Power'
1967	Supreme Court rules that laws forbidding inter-racial marriage are unconstitutional
	Thurgood Marshall becomes the first black appointed to the Supreme Court
1968	Dr. Martin Luther King assassinated

£1·95NN

Fairies

o/p

10/02

Race Relations in the United States

John Simkin

Spartacus

Contents

© Published 1988
Spartacus Educational
139 Carden Avenue, Brighton, BN1 8NH

ISBN 0 948865 28 8

Printed by Delta Press, Hove.

Background to Racial Conflict in the USA

The first black people to arrive in North America were explorers. The most famous of these was Estevanico who led the first expedition to New Mexico and Arizona. The black population of North America remained small until the development of the cotton, sugar and tobacco plantations in the seventeenth century. The owners of the plantations had difficulty in recruiting labour from the local population. Their solution to this problem was to import slaves from Africa.

The main demand for slaves came from the English colonists living in the southern areas of America. By 1754, 220,000 of the 604,000 people living in Maryland, Virginia, North Carolina, South Carolina and Georgia were black slaves. These slaves worked from sunrise to sunset and at harvest time worked an eighteen-hour day, seven day week.

The large increase in the slave population was followed by the introduction of slave codes. These were laws that only applied to slaves and were an attempt to prevent them from rebelling against slavery. Punishment for breaking these codes included branding, maiming, whipping and burning.

The northern colonies also had slaves. However, the mixed-farming economy of the North did not make slavery profitable and it gradually came to an end. By 1804 the northern states of Rhode Island, Vermont, Pennsylvania, Massachusetts, New Hampshire, Connecticut, New York and New Jersey had all abolished slavery. Although the northern blacks were free they did not have equality. The northern states passed laws that prevented blacks from voting, serving on juries, receiving an education and working in certain trades.

A small percentage of the blacks in the South were also free. Some purchased their liberty while others were given their freedom when their masters died. Free blacks living in the South were always in danger of being taken into slavery, and many moved to the relative safety of the free states in the North.

Escaped slaves also headed for the free states or Canada. It is estimated that 3,000 people were involved in helping slaves to escape to the North. The escaped slaves travelled by night

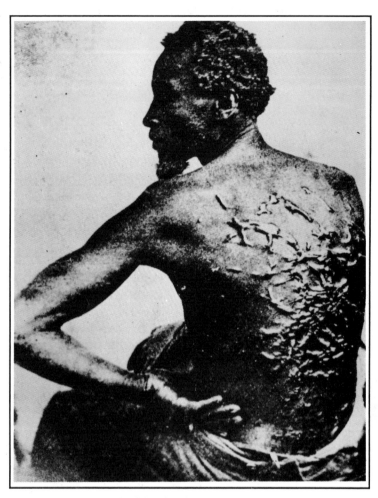

Whipped slave in 1860.

and during the day they hid in the houses of people who opposed slavery. This route became known as the 'Underground Railroad'. It has been claimed that between 1810 and 1860, approximately 175,000 slaves escaped in this way.

The conflict between the northern and southern states over the issue of slavery grew during the nineteenth century. The northern states were going through an industrial revolution and desperately needed more people to work in their factories.

Industrialists in the North believed that if freed, the slaves would leave the South and provide the necessary labour they required.

The North also wanted tariffs on imported goods to protect their new industries. The South was still mainly an agricultural economy that purchased a lot of goods from abroad and was therefore opposed to import tariffs.

The main political party in America was the pro-slavery, Democratic Party. In 1854, a group of politicians in the North formed the Republican Party. Northern industrialists, anxious for their policies to be implemented, supplied money and other forms of support for this new party.

In 1861, Abraham Lincoln, the Republican candidate, became the President of America. Although Lincoln had not proposed the abolition of slavery during the election, the southern states feared the worst when he was elected, and eleven of them decided to leave the Union and form their own Confederate government.

This decision led to the outbreak of the American Civil War. The Union consisted of 23 states and 22,000,000 people compared with only 9,000,000 people (including 3,500,000 slaves) in the Confederacy.

During the Civil War the Anti-Slavery movement urged the Union government to pass legislation that would give slaves their freedom. President Lincoln was worried about upsetting the white population in the Union that still had slaves and attempted to negotiate a system of compensation for slave-owners. Lincoln also wanted to set up a scheme whereby freed slaves could go and live in Haiti, Liberia and Panama.

In January 1863, a law was passed announcing that all slaves in the Confederate states were now free. The general reaction of white Americans in the North was hostile. Some soldiers resigned from the army complaining that the motives for the war had changed from saving the Union to ending slavery.

When the Civil War came to an end with the defeat of the Confederate forces, all slaves, including those in the North, were given their freedom. However, they were not compensated for past labour. Cast out by many plantation owners, this was a period of great suffering for black people

Harriet Tubman worked as a nurse, scout
and intelligence agent for the Union Army.

living in the South.

In 1870, the United States Congress passed the Fifteenth
Amendment. This amendment to the American Constitution
declared that the right to vote should not be denied on account
of race or colour. In states such as Alabama, Louisiana, South
Carolina, Florida and Mississippi blacks were in the majority.

Southern states began to elect black politicians. As they were usually ex-slaves they tended to be sympathetic to the poorer members of the community. Free education was introduced, and the system of having to own property before being allowed to vote was brought to an end.

In 1877, the United States army began to leave the southern states. Without the protection of federal troops, the black population in the South found themselves under attack. Secret white supremacy organisations such as the Ku Klux Klan and the Knights of the White Camelia began to use violence to keep blacks from voting. After the election of white governments, new laws were passed against black Americans. By the end of the nineteenth century the black population in America was once again firmly under the control of the white population.

Race Relations 1900-1914

After slavery had been abolished, the primary concern of the plantation owners in the South was to develop a system which would continue to provide them with cheap black labour. The main way they did this was through the share-cropping system. The cropper would be hired by the plantation owner just before the spring ploughing season, and given land, seed and farm equipment. After the harvest the black cropper would receive between one-third and one-tenth of the crop. The rest of the harvest would be taken by the plantation owner.

In many cases share-cropping proved to be more profitable to the white farmer than the old slave-system. There was no longer the need to buy slaves or pay for overseers. As the farmer kept the books, and many of the croppers could not read or write, fraud was common. Black croppers were sometimes told that the harvest had made a loss and they were in debt to the farmer. As laws were passed forbidding share-croppers in debt to leave the area, they became virtual prisoners of the plantation owner.

'Jim Crow' laws were also passed in the South to segregate the blacks from the whites. Blacks had to travel in separate compartments on trains, go to black schools and hospitals, sit at

9

the back of theatres, were buried in different cemeteries and forbidden to enter public libraries. Blacks were not allowed to enter certain restaurants, bars or hotels except when they were serving whites. Races were even segregated in church.

The low wages paid to blacks meant that they tended to live in poorer neighbourhoods. In some towns laws were passed to guarantee this segregation. All races were allowed to walk on the same pavements, but blacks always had to move to one side to allow whites to pass. Failure to do this led to blacks being whipped or lynched.

Blacks also constantly had to face racial abuse. One black writer commented: "There appears to be a fixed determination on the part of our oppressors in this country to destroy every vestige of our self-respect." Given this situation, blacks, whenever possible, tended to avoid contact with whites.

The whites were particularly concerned about mixed marriages. They feared that this would eventually lead to a society where racial categorisation would be difficult. In such a situation white dominance would be hard to maintain. Between 1870 and 1890 all southern states made inter-racial marriage illegal. By the beginning of the twentieth century all social contact between black and white was strongly discouraged. This meant that whites and blacks rarely came into personal contact except in the relationship between employer and worker.

In 1900, 95% of the black population lived in the South. Some blacks attempted to escape from racial prejudice by moving to the North. However, even though there was more mixing between the races in the North the blacks still suffered from racial discrimination. Blacks were denied work in most skilled trades and consequently they were forced to accept menial work. When blacks did find employment they were often paid lower wages than white workers. In periods of economic recession black workers were always the first to be fired.

Trade unions often refused membership to black workers. Unemployment and non-union status meant that blacks were sometimes willing to act as strike-breakers during industrial disputes. This led to even more hostility between unions and black workers.

Ku Klux Klan

The Ku Klux Klan was originally formed in 1867 by a group of ex-Confederate soldiers. They attempted to maintain 'white supremacy', which they felt was under threat after the Confederate defeat in the Civil War. In the years that followed, Klansmen, wearing masks, white cardboard hats and draped in white sheets, tortured and killed blacks in the South. White people who supported equal rights for blacks also suffered at the hands of the Ku Klux Klan.

At first, the main objective of white supremacy organisations such as the Ku Klux Klan, the White League and the Knights of the White Camelia was to stop black people from voting. After white governments had been established in the South the Ku Klux Klan continued to undermine the power of blacks. Successful black businessmen were attacked and any attempt to form black protection groups such as trade unions was quickly dealt with.

The Ku Klux Klan also became involved in lynching black people suspected of breaking the law. Lynching is the term used for the murder, usually by hanging or burning, of a person by a mob before he or she has undergone a trial. It has been estimated that between 1880 and 1920, an average of two black people per week were lynched in the United States.

The white mobs involved in lynching blacks claimed that those executed were guilty of serious crimes such as murder and rape. Research by writers at the time indicated that most of the victims were innocent or were only accused of minor offences. Ida Wells, a black newspaper editor from Memphis, kept a record for several years of all people lynched in the United States. Her research revealed that the main aim of lynching was not to punish criminals but to intimidate the local black population into accepting the total control of society by the white population.

Lynch victims and their families.

12

Booker T. Washington

Booker T. Washington was born a slave in Virginia in 1856. In 1882 he took charge of a small black school in Tuskegee, Alabama. Washington argued that black students should concentrate on vocational education instead of academic subjects. He did not believe that blacks should campaign for the vote, and claimed that blacks needed to prove their loyalty to the United States by working hard without complaint before being granted their political rights. Washington accepted segregation and tended to ignore the unfairness of the Jim Crow laws.

Southern whites, who had previously been against the education of black people, supported Washington's ideas as they saw them as a means of encouraging blacks to accept their inferior economic and social status. White businessmen donated large sums of money to his school. Tuskegee grew rapidly and soon Booker T. Washington had ten schools and 2,000 students.

White politicians were keen that Booker T. Washington should become the leader of the American black population. To help him in this white politicians had meetings with Washington to discuss political issues. In 1901, President Theodore Roosevelt invited Booker T. Washington to visit him in the White House. To southern whites this was going too far. One southern newspaper wrote: "With our long-matured views on the subject of social intercourse between blacks and whites, the least we can say now is that we deplore the President's taste, and we distrust his wisdom." Washington ignored this racism and continued to argue that it was the role of blacks to serve whites, and that those black leaders who demanded social equality were political extremists.

William Du Bois

William Du Bois was born the son of poor parents in 1868 in Massachusetts. He attended Harvard University, and in 1895 became the first black man in the United States to obtain a Ph.D. degree. Du Bois became a university lecturer who specialised in the history of Afro-Americans.

In 1905, William Du Bois helped form the Niagara Movement. This black civil rights group campaigned for freedom of speech, universal suffrage and an end to racial discrimination.

William Du Bois was strongly opposed to Washington's attempts to train blacks to accept low status occupations. As a supporter of the Niagara Movement pointed out: "White America had raised [Washington] up because he espoused a policy which intended to keep the Negro docile in regard to civil, social, and political rights and privileges."

NAACP

In 1909, Mary Ovington read an article about racial discrimination in America. She decided that there should be a nation-wide organisation supporting equal rights for black

Booker T. Washington   William Du Bois

people. Mary Ovington, who was a socialist and suffragette, contacted friends who shared her political views, and together they formed the National Association for the Advancement of Coloured People (NAACP).

The NAACP began a long legal battle against racial discrimination and lynching. They appealed to the Supreme Court to rule that several laws passed by southern states were unconstitutional. They won three important Supreme Court judgements between 1915-23 concerning voting rights and housing in the South.

The NAACP also started its own magazine, *Crisis*. The magazine was edited by William Du Bois and soon built up a large readership amongst black people and white sympathisers.

First World War

The United States declared war on Germany on April 6, 1917. President Wilson told the American people that the war was being waged to make the world more democratic. It was suggested that if blacks fought in the war they would be rewarded with the vote in America.

Approximately 2,291,000 black Americans volunteered and 367,000 of them were accepted. Most of these joined the army. The marines and the air-force refused to take black volunteers and they were only offered menial tasks in the navy.

Three-quarters of those who served in the army overseas worked as cooks, orderlies and truck drivers. The training camps were segregated and black regiments tended to have white officers.

The first black soldiers to arrive in Europe were those of the 369th Regiment from New York. The regiment quickly built up a reputation as excellent soldiers and were nicknamed the 'Hell Fighters' by the Germans. The 369th was the first Allied regiment to break through the German lines to reach the Rhine. During 191 days of fighting, the regiment did not have a man captured; nor did it lose an inch of ground by retreating. The military leaders in France were so impressed with the way they fought at the Battle of Maison-en-Champagne that they gave the regiment the Croix de Guerre medal.

The Germans were well aware of how black Americans were treated in their own country and attempted to persuade them to change sides. Propaganda leaflets informed black soldiers how many blacks had been lynched in the United States while they had been fighting in Europe. The leaflets suggested that if the black soldiers changed sides the Germans would help them in their fight for democracy and civil rights. This tactic was unsuccessful as none of the black soldiers deserted.

With workers recruited into the armed forces and the rapid growth in the armaments industry, there was a shortage of labour in the North. Employers sent labour recruiters into the South. It is estimated that between 1915 and 1918 about 500,000 black Americans were persuaded to move from the South to the northern industrial states.

Black Americans were still denied the opportunity to enter certain trades and they mainly found lower-paid jobs in ship-building, coal-mines, armaments and the railways. Employers were impressed with their hard work, and in two cases black workers broke two world records for productivity in the ship building industry.

In northern states such as New York, Illinois and Ohio, blacks were now about 5% of the voting population. This gave blacks in these states a certain amount of power, and in future politicians running for election would have to take their political views into account.

After the war had ended blacks were sacked and replaced by white soldiers returning from Europe. Tension increased between black and white workers in the North. Workers feared that the presence of blacks from the South would result in a fall in wage-rates. In 1919, a five-day race-riot took place in Chicago. Thirty-eight people were killed (15 whites and 23 blacks) and another five hundred were injured. Violence also erupted in other northern cities. A new factor was emerging in race relations in the United States; blacks in the North were no longer willing to passively accept violent attacks on them by gangs of whites. The experience of the First World War had encouraged them to fight back.

The debt owed to blacks who fought bravely in the war and

A group of white people in Chicago in July, 1919 who had just burnt down a home owned by a black family.

worked hard in the armament industries was soon forgotten. More than seventy blacks were lynched in the year after the war ended. Ten black soldiers, several still in their army uniforms, were amongst those lynched. Between 1919 and 1922, a further 239 blacks were lynched by white mobs and many more were killed by individual acts of violence and unrecorded lynchings. In none of these cases was a white person punished for these crimes.

Marcus Garvey

Marcus Garvey was born in Jamaica in 1867. He moved to the United States during the First World War where he formed the Universal Negro Improvement Association (UNIA). The organisation proved to be extremely popular with American blacks and by 1919 he had two million members.

Like the NAACP, Garvey campaigned against lynching, Jim Crow laws, denial of black voting-rights and racial discrimination. Where UNIA differed from other civil rights organisations was on how the problem could be solved. Garvey doubted whether whites in the United States would ever agree to black people being treated as equals and argued that blacks should demand complete segregation from whites. Garvey suggested that American blacks should go and live in Africa. He wrote that UNIA believed: "in the principle of Europe for the Europeans, and Asia for the Asiatics" and "Africa for the Africans at home and abroad."

Garvey began to sign up recruits who were willing to travel to Africa and "clear out the white invaders." He formed an army, equipping them with uniforms and weapons. Garvey appealed to the new militant feelings of blacks that followed the end of the First World War and asked those blacks who had been willing to fight for democracy in Europe to now join his army to fight for the black cause.

In 1919 Garvey formed the Black Cross Navigation and Trading Company. With $10,000,000 invested by his supporters Garvey purchased two steamships to take American blacks to Africa. After making a couple of journeys to Africa the Black Cross Navigation and Trading Company ran out of money. Garvey was a poor businessman and, although he was probably honest himself, several people in his company had been involved in corruption.

Garvey was arrested and charged with fraud and in 1925 was sentenced to five years imprisonment. Two years later he was released and deported to Jamaica. Garvey's efforts had ended in failure but, with his demands for segregation and his willingness to use violence to obtain black equality, he was the forerunner of the black nationalist movement that was to re-emerge after the Second World War.

The Great Depression

After the Wall Street Crash in October 1929, the United States economy went into recession. By March 1933 unemployment had reached nearly thirteen million. Black workers suffered most during the crisis. Factories sacked black workers and then gave the jobs to whites. In most areas unemployment among

blacks was twice as high as among whites. Wages fell, with blacks receiving, on average, 30% less than white workers. By 1933 over 50% of all black workers were unemployed.

The Great Depression also hurt black businesses. Of the 144 black banks established after 1888, only 12 were still operating in 1935. Many blacks who had gradually obtained good jobs through education now had to accept low-status, low-income employment.

Before the 1932 presidential election most blacks who had the vote supported the Republican Party because it had ended slavery. Mounting evidence of racial discrimination in the Republican Party and the failure of President Hoover to solve the economic crisis, resulted in the vast majority of blacks in 1932 supporting Franklin Roosevelt's promise of a New Deal.

Many aspects of the New Deal did not benefit the blacks as much as they hoped. In the South, the New Deal was administered by white officials and many blacks did not receive the benefits that were due to them. As few blacks had the vote in the South they were not a very strong political force. Roosevelt, who relied on the support of the white vote in the South, was reluctant to criticise the racial discrimination that was taking place. However, his wife, Eleanor Roosevelt, was willing to speak up on their behalf. Eleanor also attempted, without success, to persuade her husband to support an Anti-Lynching Bill that was introduced in Congress in 1935. Roosevelt refused to speak out in favour of the bill that would punish sheriffs who failed to protect their prisoners from lynch mobs. He argued that the white voters in the South would never forgive him if he supported the bill and that he would therefore lose the next presidential election.

Second World War

Black leaders in the United States were early opponents of Hitler's Nazi regime in Germany. After being on the receiving end of racism for many years, black people were fully aware of the dangers of fascism. Many blacks went to Spain in 1936 to fight for the International Brigade against Franco's fascists. For the first time American black soldiers fought in unsegregated regiments. Casualties were high and about half of the black soldiers who went to Spain were killed.

American blacks did however have two famous victories against the Nazi's belief in the superiority of the Aryan race. In the 1936 Berlin Olympic Games, the black American athlete, Jessie Owens, won a record four gold medals. Two years later, black boxer, Joe Louis, knocked out the German world heavyweight champion, Max Schmeling.

When the Second World War broke out in Europe, racial discrimination was still a common feature in the United States

Armed Forces. Regiments were still segregated and virtually all officers were white. In 1939 there were only twelve black officers in the whole of the United States Army.

The fear that the United States would soon be pulled into the Second World War resulted in a rapid increase in the size of the armed forces. This opened up employment opportunities for black workers. Even with the increased demand for labour, blacks were still prevented from obtaining certain jobs. Philip Randolph, a black trade union leader, announced a plan to organise a march of 100,000 people on Washington in protest against racial discrimination in the armaments industries. When attempts to persuade Randolph to call off the march failed, President Roosevelt issued an order in June 1941, that "there shall be no discrimination in the employment of workers in defence industries or Government because of race, creed, colour, or national origin." This was a turning-point in the history of the black race in the United States. The threat of mass action had produced results. Black leaders called it the most significant event since the end of slavery in 1865.

Black leaders then turned to racial discrimination in the armed forces and submitted a seven-point programme of reform to President Roosevelt. This was ignored, and in 1940 it was announced that segregation would continue. After protest demonstrations changes were made. It was agreed to train black pilots and to allow black men to become sailors. In 1942 the marines and the coast guard enlisted black men for the first time.

Segregation of the armed forces created organisational problems under battle conditions, and in January 1945 the United States government gave permission for black troops to be integrated with white troops when fighting abroad. The experiment was a success and senior officers praised the way that the mixed regiments performed. However, as soon as the war was over these units were broken up and the army returned to segregated regiments.

Civil Rights and the Cold War

In April 1945, a conference for the establishment of the United Nations was held in San Francisco. From these discussions emerged the United Nations Charter. Blacks in the United States were particularly happy with the passage stating that the United Nations Organisation would support "universal respect

Air-force veterans had their house fire-bombed after they moved into a mainly white residential area.

for, and observance of, human rights and fundamental freedoms for all without distinction to race, sex, language, or religion." The United States government that had been instrumental in setting up the United Nations supported these ideals.

Communist governments in Eastern Europe were especially criticised by the United States for not holding elections after the war. However, they found it extremely embarrassing when it was pointed out that these same civil rights being advocated for people living in Eastern Europe were being denied to blacks living in the United States.

Harry Truman, who had become president after Roosevelt death in 1945, announced the formation of a committee to look into the issue of civil rights in the United States. Government agencies were told to employ a higher percentage of black people, and in 1948 Truman ordered "equality of treatment and opportunity" in the armed forces.

The outbreak of the war in Korea also helped the plight of blacks in the United States. When the communists in North Korea made rapid gains in 1950, General Ridgeway, the United States Commander, was under so much pressure that he was forced to use black and white regiments together. Afterwards it was agreed that integration of the troops helped to prevent defeat and that it should remain a permanent feature of the United States armed forces.

The growth of the anti-communist hysteria that followed the Korean War also helped the black cause. It became more and more difficult for Harry Truman and his presidential successor, Dwight Eisenhower, to claim the United States was the leader in the fight against undemocratic communist forces when a considerable number of their own citizens were being denied the right to vote.

Although Truman and Eisenhower advocated black civil rights they were reluctant to force the southern states to change their policies. Like Roosevelt before them they were aware that if they did so, they faced the danger of upsetting the majority of whites in the South whose support could prove crucial in any future elections. The blacks, on the other hand, only made up 10% of the population and most of them did not have the vote.

Segregation in Education

During the 1950s the main tactic of the NAACP and other civil rights pressure groups was to use the courts to end racial discrimination in the United States. One of the objectives was to end the system of having separate schools for black and white children in the South. The states of Texas, Oklahoma, Arkansas, Missouri, Louisiana, Mississippi, Alabama, Georgia, Florida, South Carolina, North Carolina, Virginia, West Virginia and Kentucky all prohibited black and white children from going to the same school.

The NAACP appealed to the Supreme Court in 1952 to rule that school segregation was unconstitutional. The Supreme Court ruled that separate schools were acceptable as long as they were "separate and equal". It was not too difficult for the

NAACP to provide information to show that black and white schools in the South were not equal. Throughout the twentieth century southern states had spent far more on white schools. One study in 1937 for example revealed that spending on white pupils in the South was $37.87 compared to the $13.08 spent on black children. There were also fewer opportunities for black students to attend universities in the South.

In 1954 the Supreme Court announced that separate schools were not equal and ruled that they were therefore unconstitutional. Some states accepted the ruling and began to desegregate. This was especially true of states with small black populations who had found the provision of separate schools extremely expensive. However, states in the Deep South refused to accept the judgement of the Supreme Court.

In September 1957, in Little Rock, Arkansas, Governor Faubus used military force to stop black children from attending the local high school. Film of the events at Little Rock was shown throughout the world. This was extremely

damaging to the image of the United States as leader of the 'free world'. After waiting for eighteen days, President Eisenhower decided to send federal troops to Arkansas to ensure that black children could go to Little Rock's Central High School.

The white population of Little Rock were furious that they were being forced by President Eisenhower to integrate their school. Governor Faubus described the federal troops as an army of occupation. The nine black students at Little Rock Central High suffered physical violence and constant racial abuse. Although under considerable pressure to leave the school they agreed to stay. By remaining at Little Rock Central High School they showed the rest of the country that black people were determined to obtain equality.

Citizen Councils were set up all over the Deep South to resist segregation. Blacks who advocated an end to segregation in the South found themselves victimised. As an official of the Alabama Citizen Council pointed out: "The white population in this country controls the money... We intend to make it difficult, if not impossible, for any Negro who advocates desegregation to find and hold a job, get credit or renew a mortgage."

The NAACP and other black civil rights organisations continued to argue for an end to segregation but progress was slow. By 1963 only 10% of black children in the South went to desegregated schools. State Universities in the South also prevented black students from attending classes. Others let black students in but treated them so badly that they left of their own accord.

Bus Boycott In Montgomery

Segregation on buses and trains had long been a humiliating experience for black people in America. Ever since it was formed in 1908, the NAACP had appealed to the Supreme Court to take action. In 1952 segregation on inter-state railways was declared unconstitutional by the Supreme Court. This was followed in 1954 by a similar judgement concerning inter-state buses. However, states in the South continued their own policy of transport segregation. This usually involved whites sitting in the front and blacks at the back. When the bus was crowded, the rule was that blacks sitting nearest to the front had to give up their seats to any whites that were standing.

Black people who disobeyed the state's transport segregation policies were arrested and fined. On December 1, 1955, Rosa Parks, a middle-aged tailor's assistant from Montgomery, Alabama, who was tired after a hard day's work, refused to give up her seat to a white man. After her arrest, Martin Luther King, a pastor at the local Baptist Church, helped organise protests against bus segregation. It was decided that black people in Montgomery would refuse to use the buses until passengers were completely integrated. Martin Luther King was arrested and his house was fire-bombed. Others involved in the boycott also suffered from harassment and intimidation, but the protest continued.

For thirteen months the 17,000 black people in Montgomery walked to work or obtained lifts from the small car-owning

Rosa Parks on her way to the court in Montgomery.

black population of the city. Eventually, the loss of revenue and a decision by the Supreme Court forced the Montgomery Bus Company to accept integration.

Freedom Riders

Transport segregation continued in some parts of the South, so in 1961 a civil rights group, the Congress of Racial Equality (CORE) began to organise 'Freedom Rides'. After three days of training in nonviolent techniques, black and white volunteers sat next to each other as they travelled through the Deep South. Local police were unwilling to protect these passengers and in several places they were beaten up by white mobs with iron bars. Pictures of the beatings appeared on television and in the press. With the local authorities unwilling to protect the 'Freedom Riders', President Kennedy sent U.S. marshals from the North to do the job.

By the end of 1961 there were over 1,000 people involved in

Freedom Riders John Lewis and James Zwerg after being beaten up by a white mob in Montgomery, Alabama.

Freedom Rides. On their journeys they also campaigned against other forms of racial discrimination. They sat together in segregated restaurants, lunch counters and hotels. This was especially effective when it concerned large companies who, fearing boycotts in the North, began to desegregate their shops, restaurants and hotels in the South. As with the bus boycott in Montgomery and the conflict at Little Rock, the Freedom Rides had given world publicity to the racial discrimination suffered by blacks in America, and in doing so had helped to bring about change.

Martin Luther King

Martin Luther King was born in Georgia in 1929. His father and grandfather had both been Baptist preachers who had been actively involved in the civil rights movement. As a student at university he became interested in Gandhi's belief that passive resistance could be an effective method of obtaining political change. Gandhi's success in India inspired King to consider how these tactics could be used by the civil rights movement in the United States.

At the age of twenty-seven Martin Luther King became a national figure when he played a prominent role in the Montgomery bus boycott. After the successful campaign, King and two other ministers organised a conference on civil rights at Atlanta, Georgia. At this meeting it was decided to form the Southern Christian Leadership Conference (SCLC). This new organisation was committed to using nonviolence in the struggle for civil rights, and SCLC adopted the motto: "Not one hair of one head of one white person should be harmed."

There had been a long tradition of nonviolent resistance to racism in the United States. Frederick Douglass had advocated these methods during the fight against slavery. Other black leaders such as Philip Randolph and Bayard Rustin had successfully used nonviolence against racism in the 1940s. The importance of the SCLC was that now the black church, a powerful organisation in the South, was to become fully involved in the struggle for civil rights.

After the successful end to the Montgomery bus boycott,

Martin Luther King wrote a book called *Stride Toward Freedom*. The book described what happened at Montgomery and explained King's views on nonviolence and direct action. *Stride Toward Freedom* was to have a considerable influence on the civil rights movement.

In Greensboro, North Carolina, a small group of black students read the book and decided to take action themselves. They started a sit-in at the restaurant of their local Woolworth's store which had a policy of not serving black people. In the days that followed they were joined by other black students until they occupied all the seats in the restaurant. The students were often physically assaulted, but following the teachings of Martin Luther King they did not hit back. This tactic was soon adopted by black students all over the South. Within six months the sit-ins had ended restaurant and lunch-counter segregation in twenty-six southern cities. Student sit-ins were also successful against segregation in public parks, swimming-pools, theatres, churches, libraries, museums and beaches.

Students attempting to obtain service in Woolworths' white lunch-counter in Greensboro, North Carolina.

Martin Luther King travelled the country making speeches and inspiring people to become involved in the civil rights movement. He advocated direct nonviolent action such as the lunch-counter sit-ins. King also suggested economic boycotts similar to the one that took place at Montgomery. He argued that as the blacks made up 10% of the population they had considerable economic power. By selective buying, blacks could reward companies that were sympathetic to the civil rights movement while punishing those that still segregated their workforce or customers.

King also believed in the importance of the ballot. Once all the black population had the vote they would become an important political force. Although they were a minority, once the vote was organised, they could determine the result of presidential and state elections. This was illustrated by the black support for John Kennedy that helped to give him a narrow victory in the 1960 election.

In the Deep South considerable pressure was put on blacks not to vote by organisations such as the Ku Klux Klan. An example of this was the state of Mississippi. By 1960 42% of the population were black but only 2% were registered to vote. Lynching was still employed as a method of terrorising the local black population. Emmett Till, a fourteen-year-old schoolboy was lynched for whistling at a white woman, while others were murdered for encouraging black people to register to vote. Martin Luther King helped organise voting registration campaigns in states such as Mississippi but progress was slow.

Martin Luther King and other black leaders realised that only a new civil rights law would force the Deep South to treat blacks as equals. In August 1963, 250,000 people marched on Washington to demand legislation. At the end of the march King made his famous 'I Have a Dream' speech.

Congress continued to block the civil rights bill and it was only with the assassination of Kennedy that Congress, in a mood of sympathy, passed the former president's bill. The Civil Rights Act of 1964 prohibited segregation in hotels, restaurants, shops, libraries, transport and in places of recreation. The bill also attempted to make discrimination in voting or registration procedures illegal but this proved to be fairly ineffective.

Black Nationalism

Not all black civil rights activists supported Martin Luther King's views on nonviolence. The 1960s saw a re-emergence of the black nationalism first put forward by Marcus Garvey forty years previously. The new leader of this movement was Elijah Muhammad who formed an organisation called the Black Muslims. Like Garvey, Muhammad argued that whites would never treat blacks as equals and was therefore in favour of complete segregation of the races. He accepted that a return to Africa was no longer viable so instead he suggested a separate black state in America.

Muhammad pointed out that black people in the United States had originally adopted the names of their slave-owners. To show their independence of their slave past Muslims adopted the letter X as their surname.

The Black Muslims segregated themselves from the rest of

Malcolm X addressing a rally in Harlem in 1963.

American society. They educated their children in their own schools, set up their own businesses and refused to vote in elections or join the armed forces.

Muslims were especially successful at recruiting members from prisons. By 1962 over six hundred convicts had joined the organisation, including Malcolm Little, who was in prison for burglary. Malcolm X, as he became known, soon advanced up the hierarchy of the Black Muslims.

After disagreements with Elijah Muhammad, Malcolm X left the Black Muslims and in 1964 formed his own Organization of Afro-American Unity. He changed his views on the issue of segregation and began to argue in favour of joint action with white supporters of civil rights.

Malcolm X was assassinated on February 21, 1965. Three men were found guilty of his murder and although one of them admitted he was hired to kill Malcolm X, he refused to reveal who paid him the money.

In 1966, another black nationalist group, the Black Panther Party, was formed in Los Angeles. They carried guns and made aggressive speeches saying they would use violence to protect themselves. The Black Panther's talk of revolution worried the police and many of the members were arrested and sent to prison. With their leaders killed by the police, in prison or in hiding, the Black Panther Party gradually disintegrated.

Although black nationalism received considerable publicity during the 1960s, it never gained the support enjoyed by nonviolent civil rights groups. A survey carried out in 1966 showed that less than 5% of blacks approved of black nationalism whereas 60% were hostile to the idea.

Black Riots

The Civil Rights Act of 1964 was an important stage in the struggle for black equality. However, discrimination is difficult to prove and there was still considerable evidence that black people were being treated as second-class citizens. Figures showed that more black people were unemployed in 1964 than in 1954. Those in work still received lower wages than whites and the situation appeared to be getting worse. In 1950 black wages were on average only 61% of those paid to whites. By 1964 the percentage had fallen to 59%.

Low wages and unemployment forced many blacks to live in poor housing in run-down areas. Although segregation was illegal, economic factors meant that it continued. In fact research carried out in the 1960s showed that housing segregation was more common than it had been in the 1950s. Economic segregation also affected the schools children attended. One survey showed that a higher percentage of black students were in segregated schools in 1964 than was the case before the Supreme Court had ruled it unconstitutional in 1954. Black leaders began to argue that the only way to achieve school integration was to bus children from black areas to attend schools in white areas.

The conditions in the black ghettos deteriorated during the 1960s. Black youth unemployment was a particular problem. Nationally, 30% of black youths were unemployed and in some areas the figure was as high as 70%. Despair and hopelessness led to violence. Much of this was directed against other blacks in the ghetto but sometimes it was turned against the police who patrolled the area. Between 1964 and 1968, riots took place in 215 different cities.

The worst riot took place in Watts, a black ghetto in Los Angeles. The riot lasted for three days and the damage to property was calculated at $40 million. Thirty-four people were killed and another 1,032 were injured. Most of those killed in the riots were black youths. Blacks argued that police were using the riots as an excuse to terrorise and intimidate the local population. For example, in one riot in Newark, twenty of the twenty-two dead were black, including an unarmed teenager who had been shot forty-five times.

The Assassination of Martin Luther King

Martin Luther King began to direct his energies to helping those suffering from poverty. King realised that race and economic issues were closely connected and he began talking about the need to re-distribute wealth. He argued that blacks and poor whites were natural allies and if they worked

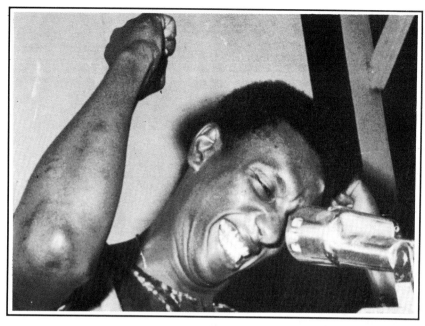

Black nationalist, Stokely Carmichael, making a speech in 1968.

together they could help change society. This point was illustrated in a speech he made in Selma, Alabama: "For the last twelve years we have been in a reform movement... [but now] we have moved into a new era, which must be an era of revolution."

The FBI became concerned about King's political development, especially when he became a strong opponent of the Vietnam War. The FBI bugged his telephones and hotel rooms and bribed King's staff into giving them information about him. Details about his private life and left-wing political friends were leaked to the press. The FBI also sent King an anonymous blackmail letter in an attempt to force him to retire from political life.

Many of King's close friends believe that these events are connected with his assassination in 1968. King was in Memphis speaking in support of low paid striking sanitation workers when he was shot allegedly by James Earl Ray. The death of Martin Luther King was followed by rioting in 125 cities and resulted in forty-six people being killed.

The right to vote in elections, established in 1965, gradually began to take effect. In 1963, there were less than 50 black elected officials in the South. By 1984, the number had grown to 3,498. Black mayors governed 255 cities, including the South's three major cities, Atlanta, New Orleans and Birmingham. There were also 21 blacks in the House of Representatives.

By the 1980s 9% of all registered voters were black. This enabled the black politician Jessie Jackson to mount a strong campaign to become the Democratic presidential candidate in 1988. Jackson, who eventually came second to Michael Dukakis, was then in a position to become involved in determining the policies of the Democratic party. In recent presidential elections the black vote has often proved vitally important in determining the result. Candidates are fully aware of this and to be successful they have to take into account the needs of the black voters. With the black vote becoming more organised it may not be too long before Martin Luther King's dream becomes a reality.

Source Material

Lynching in the Deep South

(A1) Ho Chi Minh was born in Vietnam. He became a sailor and on his travels visited the United States. He was shocked by the way that the whites treated the blacks there and in 1924 wrote an article about lynching for a French magazine. Ho Chi Minh was later to become the communist leader of North Vietnam.

Imagine a furious horde. Fists clenched, eyes bloodshot, mouths foaming, yells, insults, curses... This horde is transported with the wild delight of a crime to be committed without risk. They are armed with sticks, torches, revolvers, ropes, knives, scissors, daggers, in a word with all that can be used to kill or wound...

In a wave of hatred and bestiality, the lynchers drag the black to a wood or a public place. They tie him to a tree, pour keresene over him...

'Light up', shouts someone... The black is roasted, browned, burnt. But he deserves to die twice instead of once. He is therefore hanged, or more exactly, what is left of the corpse is hanged. And all those who were not able to help with the cooking applaud.

When everybody has had enough, the corpse is brought down. The rope is cut into small pieces which will be sold for three or five dollars each. Souvenirs and lucky charms quarrelled over by ladies...

From 1889 to 1919, 2,600 blacks were lynched, including 51 women and girls and ten former Great War soldiers...

Among the charges brought against the victims of 1919, we note: one of having distributed revolutionary publications; one of expressing his opinion on lynchings too frequently; one of having been known as a leader of the cause of the blacks; one for not getting out of the way and thus frightening a white child who was in a motor car...

In 30 years, 708 whites, including 11 women, have been lynched. Some for having organised strikes, others for having espoused the cause of the blacks.

(A2) Thomas Dixon's book *The Clansman* was published in 1902. The book portrays the Ku Klux Klan as saving the South from black rule. In 1914 D. W. Griffith, the son of a Confederate officer, made a film based on this best-selling novel and called it *The Birth of a Nation.* The NAACP, fearing that the film would incite racial hatred, attempted to have it banned. They failed and the film turned out to be the first Hollywood 'blockbuster'. The film cost $110,000 to make and took $60,000,000 at the box-office. The years that followed saw a rapid increase in the membership of the Ku Klux Klan. The still above shows a black man, accused of trying to molest a white woman, about to be lynched by the Ku Klux Klan.

(A3) This report of a lynching appeared in the *Vicksburg Evening Post,* Mississippi, on May 4, 1919.

All social classes, women and children, were present at the scene. Many ladies of high society followed the crowd from outside the prison, others joined in from neighbouring terraces... When the Negro's corpse fell, the pieces of rope were hotly contended for.

(A4) *The Charleston* was a popular newspaper with the black population in South Carolina. In 1918 the black editor of the newspaper wrote an article on the subject of lynching.

There is scarcely a day that passes that newspapers don't tell about a Negro soldier lynched in his uniform. Why do they lynch Negroes, anyhow? With a white judge, a white jury, white public sentiment, white officers of law, it is impossible for a Negro accused of a crime, or even suspected of a crime, to escape a white man's vengeance or his justice.

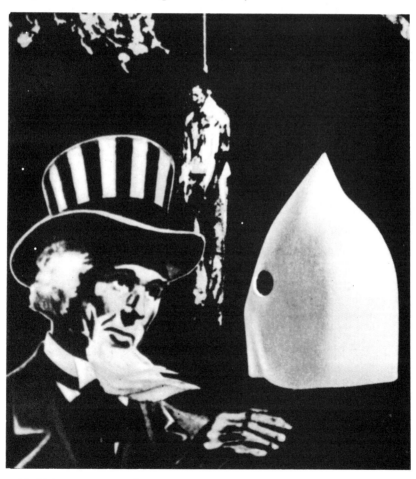

(A5) Photomontage that appeared in a magazine in the Soviet Union

(A6) Photomontage that appeared in a magazine in the Soviet Union

(A7) In 1930, Dr. Arthur Raper was appointed chief of research and investigation for the *Southern Commission on the Study of Lynching*. His report was published three years later.

3,724 people were lynched in the United States from 1889 through to 1930. Over four-fifths of these were Negroes, less than one-sixth of whom were accused of rape. Practically all of the lynchers were native whites... The fact that a number of the victims were tortured, mutilated, dragged, or burned suggests the presence of sadistic tendencies among the lynchers... Of the tens of thousands of lynchers and onlookers, only 49 were indicted and only 4 have been sentenced.

(A8) In 1981, Michael Donald, a 19-year-old black man, was lynched in Mobile, Alabama. Local police were at first unsuccessful in finding those responsible. Black politicians and lawyers demanded that the FBI look into the murder. They agreed and eventually a local man, Tiger Knowles confessed to the murder.

I know that people tried to discredit my testimony... I've lost my family. I've got people after me now. Everything I said is true... I was acting as a Klansman when I did this and I hope that people learn from my mistake... I do hope you decide a judgement against me and everyone else involved.

(A9) Tiger Knowles was found guilty of violating Michael Donald's civil rights and was sentenced to life imprisonment. Another member of the Ku Klux Klan, Henry Hays, was found guilty of murder and sentenced to death. Information that came out during the trial led to Henry's father, Bennie Hays, the leader of the Ku Klux Klan in Alabama, also being arrested for the murder. The dead boy's mother, Beulah Donald, decided to take the issue further and sued the Ku Klux Klan for the loss of her son.

In February 1987, an all-white jury in Mobile needed to deliberate only four hours before awarding her $7 million. In May, the Klan turned over the deed to its only significant asset, the $225,000 national headquarters building in Tuscaloosa. Meanwhile, Mrs Donald's attorney moved to seize the property and stop the wages of individual defendants. "The Klan, at this point, is washed up," said Henry Hays from his cell on death row.

Questions

1. Explain what is meant in source A1 by: (i) "Great War soldiers"; (ii)"distributed revolutionary publications"; (iii) "espoused the cause of blacks".

2. Do sources A3 and A7 confirm or contradict source A1? Select passages from the sources to illustrate your answer.

3. (a) What does source A1 tell us about the attitude of the writer towards lynching? (b) How does this help to explain the reasons why he wrote the article?

4. What question does the author of source A4 ask? Why does he ask this question? Use information from other sources in this unit to supply an answer to this question.

5. Explain the meaning of sources A5 and A6. Why were these pictures more likely to appear in magazines in the Soviet Union than in the United States?

6. Sources can be used as evidence in different ways. Comment on the usefulness of the film *Birth of a Nation* to a historian writing about: (i) the history of lynching; (ii) the growth of the Ku Klux Klan; (iii) Hollywood's portrayal of black people.

7. What evidence is there in sources A8 and A9 that attitudes towards lynching have changed in the United States in the last eighty years? Give as many reasons as you can why this has happened.

8. With reference to the sources in this unit, explain why historians are interested in the origin of the sources they use.

Jim Crow Laws

(B1) Ida Wells was born a slave in Mississippi in 1862. After working as a schoolteacher, Ida became the editor of the *Memphis Free Speech* newspaper. Throughout her life Ida Wells campaigned against racial discrimination. She travelled the world making speeches on the subject. The following passage is from a letter she wrote to a British newspaper, the *Daily Post*.

In the ten years succeeding the Civil War thousands of Negroes were murdered for the crime of casting a ballot. As a consequence their vote is entirely nullified throughout the entire South. The laws of the Southern states make it a crime for whites and Negroes to inter-marry or even ride in the same railway carriage. Both crimes are punishable by fine and imprisonment. The doors of churches, hotels, concert halls and reading rooms are alike closed against the Negro as a man, but every place is open to him as a servant.

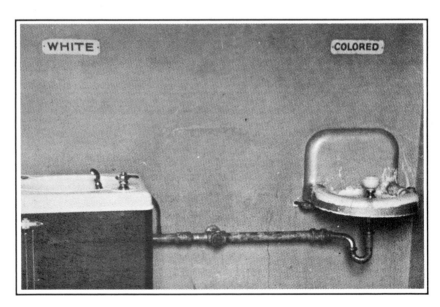

(B2) Water fountains in a town in the Deep South.

(B3) Soldiers from the 369th Infantry
Regiment wearing the Croix de Guerre.

(B4) During the First World War Germany dropped leaflets from planes on black regiments from the United States.

What is democracy? Personal freedom, all citizens enjoying the same rights socially and before the law. Do you enjoy the same rights as the white people in America, the land of Freedom and Democracy, or are you rather not treated over there as a second-class citizen? Can you go into a restaurant where white people dine? Can you get a seat in the theatre where white people sit?... Is lynching a lawful proceeding in a democratic country?

(B5) *Crisis* **was a newspaper owned by the NAACP. In May 1919, its editor, William Du Bois, wrote an article about black soldiers returning from the First World War.**

Against the threat of German race arrogance, we fought gladly and to the last drop of blood; for America and her highest ideals, we fought in far off hope... This country of ours is a shameful land.

It lynches. And lynching is a barbarism of a degree of contemptible nastiness unparalleled in human history. Yet for 50 years we have lynched two Negroes a week, and we have kept this up right through the war.

It disfranchises its own citizens. Disfranchisement is the deliberate theft and robbery of the only protection of poor against rich and black against white. The land that disfranchises its citizens and calls itself a democracy lies and knows it lies.

It encourages ignorance... It steals from us... It insults us... This is the country to which we Soldiers of Democracy return. This is the fatherland for which we fought! But it is our fatherland. It was right of us to fight... But by the God of Heaven, we are cowards and jackasses if now that the war is over, we do not marshal every ounce of our brain and brawn to fight a sterner, longer, more unending battle against the forces of hell in our own land.

We return. We return from fighting. We return fighting. Make way for Democracy! We saved it in France, and we will save it in the United States.

(B6) Richard Wright was born in Mississippi in 1908. At the age of fifteen he moved to Chicago. In 1939 he wrote an autobiographical novel, *12 Million Black Voices*. In the following passage he describes his arrival in Chicago.

We see white men and women get on the train, dressed in expensive new clothes. We look at them guardedly and wonder will they bother us. Will they ask us to stand up while they sit down? Will they tell us to go to the back of the coach? Even though we have been told that we need not be afraid, we have lived so long in fear of all white faces that we cannot help but sit and wait. We look around the train and we do not see the old familiar signs: FOR COLOURED and FOR WHITE...

Then we board our first Yankee streetcar to go to a cousin's home. We pay the conductor our fare and look about apprehensively for a seat. We have been told that we can sit where we please, but we are still scared. We cannot shake off 300 years of fear in three hours. We ease into a seat and look out of the window at the crowded streets. A white man or a white woman comes and sits besides us, not even looking at us, as though this were a normal thing to do. The muscles of our bodies tighten. Indefinable sensations crawl over our skins and our blood tingles. Out of the corners of our eyes we try to get a glimpse of the strange white face that floats but a few inches from ours.

(B7) Vending-machine in Jackson, Tennessee.

Questions

1. Explain what is meant in source B1 by: (i) "casting a ballot"; (ii) "inter-marry".

2. Study sources B1, B2, B3, B5 and B7. Explain the different ways that black people suffered from racial discrimination in the United States.

3. Why was source B4 written? Would an historian find this source useful?

4. How do sources B3, B4 and B5 help to explain why black people became more angry about racial discrimination after 1918?

5. The person who took the photograph of the Coca-Cola vending machine was arrested. Can you explain why?

6. What evidence is there in source B6 that Chicago did not have Jim Crow laws?

7. How might a black man or woman who lived in Chicago all of his or her life have reacted to the situation described in sources B1 and B6?

8. Who of the following was most likely to have said: "black people prefer to have separate facilities from whites." (i) a black woman from Chicago; (ii) a white woman from New York; (iii) a black man from Mississippi; (iv) a white man from Tennessee?

9. "Black and white people in the United States lived completely separate lives between 1900 and 1950." Do the sources in this unit show this to be true? Explain your answer fully.

Nonviolent Civil Disobedience

(C1) When Martin Luther King was at University he heard a lecture on Mahatma Gandhi and the nonviolent civil disobedience campaign that he had used successfully against British rule in India. King read several books on the ideas of Gandhi, and eventually became convinced that the same methods could be employed by blacks to obtain civil rights in America. He was particularly struck by Gandhi's words: "Through our pain we will make them see their injustice". Below is a selection of comments made by King on the subject of nonviolent civil disobedience.

(i) Privileged groups rarely give up their privileges without strong resistance... Hence the basic question which confronts the world's oppressed is: How is the struggle against the forces of injustice to be waged?... The alternative to violence is nonviolence resistance... The nonviolent resister must often express his protest through noncooperation or boycotts, but he realizes that noncooperation and boycotts are not ends in themselves; they are merely means to awaken a sense of moral shame in the opponent. (*Christian Century Magazine*, 1957)

(ii) The nonviolent resister does not seek to humiliate or defeat the opponent but to win his friendship and understanding. (speech, 1957)

(iii) Violence, even in self-defence, creates more problems than it solves. Only a refusal to hate or kill can put an end to the chain of violence in the world. (*Ebony Magazine*, 1966)

(iv) We would march until we faced the troopers. We would not disengage until they made clear that they were going to use force. We would disengage then, having made our point, revealing the continued presence of violence, and showing clearly who are the oppressed and who are the oppressors. (*Behind the Selma March*, 1965)

(v) Nonviolent direct action enabled the Negro to take to the streets in active protest, but muzzled the guns of the oppressor because even he could not shoot down in daylight unarmed men, women and children. This is the reason why there was less loss of life in ten years of southern protest than in ten days of northern riots. (*Look Magazine*, 1968)

(C2) Sit-down protest against racial discrimination.

(C3) On May 31, 1963, the *New York Times* reported on the training that young volunteers were receiving in their attempts to end racial segregation in restaurants and lunch-counters. Mr. Dennis, the teacher, was at the time the director for the Congress of Racial Equality (CORE) in Mississippi.

Mr. Dennis emphasized the need for a relaxed attitude during the demonstrations. "Don't tense or you will get the full impact of the blows," he said.

Joan Trumpauer, the second white girl, asked: "What if someone comes at you from behind?" Miss Trumpauer, a student at Tougaloo College, was one of the sit-in demonstrators who was covered with ketchup and mustard on Tuesday by a white crowd during a three-hour clash at the F.W. Woolworth Company.

"If he comes from behind," Mr. Dennis said, "you have to hope and pray that you reach that man's conscience before it's too late."

Some of them stirred restlessly, and Mr. Dennis addressed himself to them.

"We're trying to change a system with love and understanding," he said. "It's very difficult. Maybe it sounds stupid, but if any of you know what violence will accomplish, let me know."

(C4) Photograph of Martin Luther King in his office.

(C5) James Peck became a pacifist while at Harvard University in the 1930s. In the 1947 he joined the Congress of Racial Equality (CORE) and received training in nonviolent techniques. During the next fifteen years, Peck, a white man, was beaten up several times while campaigning for black civil rights. In 1961 he was nearly killed by a white mob in Birmingham, Alabama.

I had been beaten almost to death by a Birmingham mob for the "crime" of trying to eat with a Negro at the terminal lunchroom... Reporters asked... "How could you take such a beating without fighting back?" I have found that the impulse to retaliate with physical violence can be curbed through a complete realization of its futility. Anger is a natural response to the physical pain resulting from assault. But when I am attacked, my reaction has come to be a sick feeling inside, a sort of overpowering nausea caused by the spectacle of physical violence. During beatings I have attempted to cover my head with my arms as best I could until the hatred of my assailants was expended... On every occasion I felt that my remaining nonviolent had proved worth while.

(C6) The Black Muslims were critical of Martin Luther King's views on nonviolence. Here are a selection of comments on the subject by Malcolm X, one of the leaders of the Black Muslims.

(i) The White man pays Reverend Martin Luther King... so that he can continue to teach the Negroes to be defenceless - that's what you mean by non-violent - be defenceless in the face of one of the most cruel beasts that has ever taken people into captivity (television interview in 1963).

(ii) I don't go along with any kind of nonviolence unless everybody's going to be nonviolent. If they make the Ku Klux Klan nonviolent, I'll be nonviolent (speech, December, 1964).

(iii) It (nonviolence) would be like putting handcuffs on me and putting me in the ring and telling me to fight Cassius Clay, or Sonny Liston, nonviolently... I think people who tell our people to be nonviolent are almost agents of the Ku Klux Klan (speech, January, 1965).

(C7) Martin Luther King being arrested in Montgomery, Alabama. Between 1956 and 1964 King was arrested ten times and spent several spells in prison.

(C8) In November, 1962, Martin Luther King was arrested and sent to prison for demonstrating against segregation in Birmingham, Alabama. While he was in prison King was criticised by a group of clergymen from Alabama who described him as a political extremist. King wrote a letter to the clergymen explaining his actions.

I was initially disappointed at being categorized as an extremist, as I continued to think about the matter I gradually gained a measure of satisfaction from the label. Was not Jesus an extremist... an extremist for love, truth and goodness.

There are two types of laws: just and unjust... One has not only a legal but a moral responsibility to obey just laws. Conversely, one has a moral responsibility to disobey unjust laws... We should never forget that everything Adolf Hitler did in Germany was "legal"... Any law that degrades human personality is unjust. All segregation statutes are unjust because segregation distorts the soul and damages the personality. It gives the segregator a false sense of superiority and the segregated a false sense of inferiority...

I submit that an individual who breaks a law that conscience tells him is unjust, and who willingly accepts the penalty of imprisonment in order to arouse the conscience of the community over its injustice, is in reality expressing the highest respect for law. Of course, there is nothing new about this kind of civil disobedience... It was practiced superbly by the early Christians, who were willing to face hungry lions and the excruciating pain of chopping blocks rather than submit to certain unjust laws of the Roman Empire.

(C9) Benjamin Hooks became executive director of the NAACP in 1977. In an interview on television three years later he explained why the NAACP was against using violence to obtain civil rights.

There are a lot of ways an oppressed people can rise... One way to rise is to study, to be smarter than your oppressor... The concept of rising against oppression through physical contact is stupid and self-defeating. It exalts brawn over brain... And the most enduring contributions made to civilisation have not been made by brawn, they have been made by brain.

Questions

1. Explain what is meant in source C1 by: (i) "nonviolent resistance"; (ii) "boycotts"; (iii) "disengage".

2. Look at source C2. What is likely to happen next? How were these events likely to help them achieve their demands?

3. Why was it necessary for members of CORE to undergo the training described in source C3?

4. What do sources C4 and C7 tell us about the views of Martin Luther King?

5. How does the fact that blacks in the United States only make up about 10% of the population help to explain the arguments being put forward in source C9?

6. What evidence is there in source C8 that Martin Luther King's political ideas were influenced by his religious beliefs?

7. Explain how Martin Luther King defends his willingness to break the law. What arguments might the Alabama clergymen have used in their reply to this letter?

8. Employ the sources in this unit to construct a debate on civil rights between a supporter of Martin Luther King and a Black Muslim.

Little Rock, Arkansas

(D1) Senator James Eastland of Mississippi made a speech on the subject of racial segregation in the United States Senate on May 27, 1954.

Separation promotes racial harmony. It permits each race to follow its own pursuits, to develop its own culture, its own institution, and its own civilisation. Segregation is not discrimination. Segregation is not a badge of racial inferiority... Segregation is desired and supported by the vast majority of the members of both of the races in the South, who dwell side by side under harmonious conditions... It is the law of nature, it is the law of God, that every race has both the right and the duty to perpetuate itself... Free men have the right to send their children to schools of their own choosing, free from governmental interference.

(D2) In 1946, President Truman established a committee on civil rights. The committee's report, published in 1947, revealed differences between black and white schools in the South. The committee pointed out that black schools had an average class size of 34 compared to 28 students per class in white schools. There was also a difference in the average wages for teachers in black and white schools (figures in $).

State	White Schools	Black Schools
Alabama	1,158	661
Arkansas	924	555
Florida	3,530	970
Georgia	1,123	515
Louisiana	1,683	828
Mississippi	1,107	342
South Carolina	1,203	615
Texas	1,395	946

(D3) Poster that was often seen in the Deep South during the 1950s.

(D4) In 1954 the Supreme Court ruled that racial segregation in state schools was unconstitutional. Black students who attempted to enter schools in the Deep South previously kept for white students were often physically attacked. Martin Luther King wrote an article explaining why school integration was important.

A demonstration against the evil of school segregation is based on the awareness that a child's mind is crippled daily by inadequate opportunity. The demonstrator agrees that it is better for him to suffer publicly for a short time to end the crippling evil of school segregation than to have generation after generation of children suffer in ignorance.

(D5) Elizabeth Eckford attempting to enter Little Rock School.

(D6) Arkansas was considered one of the moderate states in the South. By 1957 it had desegregated its buses and its State University. The Arkansas School Board also planned to slowly desegregate its schools. Nine black students were selected to go to Little Rock Central High School. Governor Orval Faubus, under pressure from segregationists, announced that he would send soldiers to Little Rock with instructions to stop black students from entering the school. On September 5, the first day of term, eight of the black students were stopped at the front gates and sent home. Elizabeth Eckford, who was late, arrived at school on her own.

I saw a large crowd of people standing across the street from the soldiers guarding Central High School... The crowd moved in closer and then began to follow me, calling me names. I still wasn't afraid. Just a little bit nervous. Then my knees started to shake all of a sudden and I wondered whether I could make it to the entrance...

When I was able to steady my knees, I walked up to the guard who had let the white students in. When I tried to squeeze past him, he raised his bayonet and then the other guards closed in and they raised their bayonets. They glared at me with a mean look and I was very frightened and didn't know what to do. I turned around and the crowd came toward me. Somebody started yelling 'Lynch her!'

I tried to find a friendly face somewhere in the mob. I looked into the face of an old woman and it seemed a kind face, but when I looked at her again she spat on me.

They came closer, shouting, 'No, nigger bitch is going to get in our school! Get out of here!' Then I saw a bench at the bus stop. When I got there, I don't think I could have gone another step. I sat down and the mob crowded up and began shouting all over again. Just then a white man sat down beside me, put his arm round me and patted my shoulder. He raised my chin and said, 'Don't let them see you cry'.

(D7) On September 24, 1957 black students entered Little Rock Central High School for the first time. The New York Times **reported the events outside the gates of the school.**

A man yelled: "Look, they're going into our school."

Six girls and three boys crossed over into the school yard. They had arrived in two automobiles and had driven to the side of the school. Mrs. Bates (President of the Arkansas Branch of the NAACP) accompanied them.

The crowd now let out a roar of rage. "They've gone in," a man shouted.

"Oh, God," said a woman, "the niggers are in school."

A group of six girls, dressed in skirts and sweaters, hair in pony-tails, started to shriek and wail.

"The niggers are in our school," they howled hysterically...

Hysteria swept from the shrieking girls to members of the crowd. Women cried hysterically, tears running down their faces.

(D8) An angry white mob surrounded the Little Rock Central High School after the nine students had gone in. Afraid that the students would be lynched, the local police arranged for them to be smuggled out of the school. That night President Eisenhower made a statement to the people of the United States. He explained that he intended sending federal troops to Little Rock to enforce the decision made by the Supreme Court in 1954.

Mob rule cannot be allowed to override the decisions of our courts... At a time when we face grave situations abroad because of the hatred that communism bears toward a system of government based on human rights, it would be difficult to exaggerate the harm that is being done to the prestige and influence, and indeed to the safety, of our nation and the world. Our enemies are gloating over this incident and using it everywhere to misrepresent our whole nation. We are portrayed as a violator of those standards of conduct which the peoples of the world united to proclaim in the Charter of the United Nations.

(D9) On September 27, with troops protecting the black students, the *New York Times* described what was going on inside Little Rock Central High School.

The Negro students in the classrooms were a novelty. And from time to time, groups of students threw down their books and walked out of the school. Some of them were chanting sing-song words that went "two four six eight, we don't want to integrate."

Many classes were half empty. Segregationist leaders had called for a student boycott. It was partly successful. Seven hundred and fifty of the 2,000 students remained away. However, the school officials thought that this might have been from fear rather than sympathy with the boycott movement...

"If the parents would just go home and leave us be," a senior, who wants to do research said, "we'd work this thing out for ourselves."

"It is just the idea of going to school with coloured kids that's hard to take at first," a boy of 17 remarked. "Once you get used to the idea it's not too bad."

"Things would be better if only the grown-ups wouldn't mix in," said (black student) Ernest Green, 16, whose ambition is to get a college education. "The kids have nothing against us. They hear bad things about us from their parents."

(D10) Troops escort nine black students into Little Rock School.

(D11) Melba Pattillo Beals was one of the nine black students at Little Rock Central High School in 1957. In 1986 she was interviewed for the television documentary *Eyes on the Prize*.

The troops were wonderful but they couldn't be with us everywhere. They couldn't be with us in the ladies bathroom. They couldn't be with us in the gym. You would be walking out to the volley-ball court and they would break a bottle and trip you over. I still have scars on my right knee from that... All the time you thought about what they were going to hit you with today. Is it going to be hot soup and will it be so greasy that it will ruin the dress my grandmother made for me... When the year ended I could have gone on for five more years because it didn't matter anymore. I was past feeling. I was into that kind of numb pain when you say: 'Do whatever you like, it just doesn't matter anymore.' I came home and by myself I went to the backyard and burnt my books and just stood by the fire and cried.

(D12) Little Rock Central High School after integration.

(D13) Mary Ellison, a lecturer in American history at Keele University, wrote a book entitled *The Black Experience* about the struggle for civil rights. In the book she considered the changing attitudes on segregation.

In 1956 only 14 per cent of white Southerners accepted integration but by 1963 that proportion had risen to between 30 and 54 per cent in those areas where considerable integration had occurred. Between December 1963 and June 1965 the Southerners shifted their attitudes to school integration in a dramatic way. Whereas in 1963 it had been favoured by only 30 per cent, in 1965 55 per cent found the idea acceptable.

Questions

1. Explain what is meant in source D1 by: (i) "racial harmony"; (ii)"segregation is not discrimination"; (iii) "free from government interference".

2. Does the information in source D2 confirm or contradict the points being made in source D4?

3. "The photograph of Elizabeth Eckford (D5) is more useful to the historian than the poster in source D3, because the poster is biased." Do you agree with this statement?

4. How would you describe the behaviour of the people outside the Little Rock Central High School in sources D6 and D7? What does the behaviour tell us about their attitudes towards black people?

5. Give two reasons why President Eisenhower decided to send federal troops to Little Rock to enforce the decision made by the Supreme Court in 1954.

6. Study sources D5, D10 and D12. Write captions for these three photographs that might have appeared in (i) a pro-segregationist newspaper in Alabama; (ii) an anti-segregationist newspaper in New York.

7. After a few weeks at Little Rock Central High School several of the black students said they wanted to return to black schools. (i) How do the sources in this unit help to explain why they wanted to leave Little Rock Central High School? (ii) What kind of arguments would Daisy Bates of the NAACP have put forward in an effort to persuade them to stay?

8. Study source D9. (i) Select two statements that are facts. (ii) Select two statement that are opinions.

9. With reference to the sources in this unit try to explain the changes in attitude towards school integration identified in source D13.

Segregation and Public Transport

(E1) Martin Luther King was a church minister in Montgomery, Alabama in 1955. In his book, *Stride Toward Freedom: The Montgomery Story*, King describes how racial segregation was organised on the buses in Alabama.

Frequently Negroes paid their fare at the front door, and then were forced to get off and reboard at the rear... An even more humiliating practice was the custom of forcing Negroes to stand over empty seats reserved for "whites only." Even if the bus had no white passengers, and Negroes were packed throughout, they were prohibited from sitting in the front four seats (which held ten persons). But the practice went further. If white persons were already occupying all of their reserved seats and additional white people boarded the bus. Negroes sitting in the unreserved section immediately behind the whites were asked to stand so that the whites could be seated. If the Negroes refused to stand and move back, they were arrested.

(E2) A bus in Montgomery, Alabama during the rush-hour.

(E3) Rosa Parks having her fingerprints taken at the police station.

(E4) Rosa Parks was a tailor's assistant in Birmingham, Alabama. In a television interview in 1979 Rosa Parks explained what happened when she caught the bus on the way home from work on December 1, 1955.

I was working in the men's alteration department at the Montgomery Fair Store, and it was leading up to the Christmas holidays. The work was quite heavy... I felt some nagging pain around the neck and shoulders and I was generally weary... When I got in the bus there was no room in the back of the bus up to where we could sit. But there was one vacant seat. I was pretty glad to get the seat... There were a few vacancies in the very front of the bus, in the white section. At the next stop a few people got on and there were no more vacancies. We went on to the third stop and several white people got on, and one white man was standing, and the driver noticed him standing. Of course, the passenger himself didn't do anything but just find a place to stand. He didn't request a seat. But the driver didn't want to see this white person stand up... Then he said, "You all better make it light on yourselves and give me those seats." At this point the man next to the window in the seat with me stood up, and the two women across the aisle stood up, but I refused to stand. The driver asked me if I was going to stand, and I said, no, I wasn't. Then he said, "If you don't stand up. I'll call the police and have you arrested."

(E5) After blacks had boycotted the buses for over a year the Montgomery Bus Company agreed to integration. When he heard the news Martin Luther King wrote a leaflet to be given out to black passengers.

Remember that this is not a victory for Negroes alone, but for all Montgomery and the South. Do not boast! Do not brag! Be quiet but friendly; proud but not arrogant. Be loving enough to absorb evil and understanding enough to turn an enemy into a friend... If there is violence in word or deed it must not be our people who commit it.

(E6) In 1961 the Congress of Racial Equality (CORE) began organising Freedom Rides. This involved black and white people breaking Jim Crow laws by sitting together on buses while travelling through the Deep South. James Peck was a white man who travelled on these buses. Here he describes what happened in Alabama on May 14, 1961.

When the Greyhound bus pulled into Anniston, it was immediately surrounded by an angry mob armed with iron bars. They set about the vehicle, denting the sides, breaking windows, and slashing tires. Finally, police arrived and the bus managed to depart. But the mob pursued in cars... Within minutes, the pursuing mob was hitting the bus with iron bars. The rear window was broken and a bomb was hurled inside...

All the passengers managed to escape before the bus burst into flames and was totally destroyed... Policemen, who had been standing by, belatedly came on the scene. A couple of them fired into the air. The mob dispersed and the injured were taken to a local hospital. (The Freedom Riders were then taken by another bus to Birmingham.)

Upon arrival in Birmingham I could see a mob lined up on the sidewalk only a few feet from the loading platform. Most of them were young - in their twenties. Some were carrying ill-concealed iron bars. All had hate showing on their faces.

I looked at them and then I looked at Charles Person, who had been designated as my team mate to test the lunch counter... When I looked at him, he responded by saying simply, "Let's go." As we entered the white waiting room and approached the lunch counter, we were grabbed bodily and pushed toward the alleyway leading to the loading platform. As soon as we got into the alleyway and out of sight of onlookers in the waiting room, six of them started swinging at me with fists and pipes. Five others attacked Person a few feet ahead. Within seconds, I was unconscious on the ground.

(E7) King and Glen Smiley travelling on a bus in Montgomery.

(E8) A bus carrying Freedom Riders fire-bombed in Alabama.

(E9) Frederick Leonard was in the second Freedom Ride bus. In an interview he gave on television in 1986 he explained what happened when the bus arrived in Montgomery, Alabama.

We went out of the front of the bus. Jim Zwerg was a white fellow from Madison, Wisconsin. He had a lot of nerve. I think that's what saved me because Jim Zwerg walked off the bus in front of us. The crowd was possessed. They couldn't believe that there was a white man who would help us. They grabbed him and pulled him into the mob. Their attention was on him. It was as if they didn't see us.

(E10) Jim Zwerg was badly injured and left in the road for over an hour. White ambulances refused to take him to hospital. Afterwards Zwerg was interviewed in hospital by reporters.

Segregation must be stopped. It must be broken down. Those of us on the Freedom Ride will continue... No matter what happens we are dedicated to this. We will take the beatings. We are willing to accept death. We are going to keep going until we can ride anywhere in the South.

(E11) James Farmer was the director of the Congress of Racial Equality and was the main organiser of the Freedom Rides. In Plaquemine, Louisiana he was surrounded by a white mob who claimed they intended to lynch him.

I was certain I was going to die. What kind of death would it be? Would they mutilate me first? What does it feel like to die? Then I grew panicky about the insurance. Had I paid the last installment? How much was it... My wife and little girls - how would it be for them?... Well, damn it, if I had to die, at least let the organisation wring some use out of my death. I hoped the newspapers were out there. Plenty of them. With plenty of cameras.

Questions

1. Use sources E1 and E4 to explain how bus segregation worked in Montgomery.
2. Study sources E2, E3 and E7. Place the three photographs in the order tn which you think they were taken. Explain why you have decided on this order.
3. Give as many reasons as you can why Martin Luther King wrote source E5.
4. The decision by Rosa Parks not to stand up on December 1, 1955 has been called one of the most significant events in the history of the United States. Why are some historical events more important than others?
5. What do sources E6, E9, E10 and E11 tell us about the attitudes of the people who travelled on the Freedom Rides in 1961?
6. It has been claimed that James Peck and Jim Zwerg suffered more from the white mobs because they were white and lived in the North. Try to explain why this should be.
7. What are the advantages and disadvantages of an eyewitness account reported at the time of the event (E10) and an eyewitness account published a few years later (E6, E9 and E11)?
8. "The photograph in source E8 is more reliable than the eyewitness accounts of the Freedom Rides because the photograph is not biased." Do you agree with this statement?
9. Identify other kinds of primary evidence that you might consult when studying the attempts by the civil rights movement to end bus segregation.

Voting Registration Campaign

(F1) White politicians in the Deep South tended to be opposed to black people voting in elections.

I want to make it absolutely impossible for the Negro to vote... and thus guarantee white supremacy. (Senator Theodore Bilbo, Mississippi, 1940)
The Ku Klux Klan is needed today as never before and I am anxious to see its rebirth in West Virginia. (Senator Robert Byrd, West Virginia, 1946)
The mental level of those people renders them incapable of suffrage. (Senator James Eastland, Mississippi, 1947)
In South Carolina, Negroes are voting in large numbers. Of course, they are not so well qualified as are the white people. (Senator Storm Thurmond, South Carolina, 1957)

(F2) In 1964, 650 members of the Student Nonviolent Coordinating Committee went to Mississippi to help black people register to vote. One student wrote to his parents explaining what happened in the county of Mileston when they attempted to help blacks register.

We got about 14 Negroes to go to the court house with the intention of registering to vote. Sheriff Smith greeted the party with a six shooter drawn from his pocket, and said "Okay, who's first?" Most of the Negroes remained cautiously quiet. After several seconds a man who had never before been a leader stepped up to the Sheriff, smiled and said, "I'm first, Hartman Turnbow." All registration applications were permitted to be filled out and all were judged illiterate. The next week, Turnbow's house was bombed with Molotov cocktails. When the Turnbow left the burning house, they were shot at... A couple of days later... Turnbow was accused of having bombed his own house which wasn't insured. Sheriff Smith was the one witness against them. Mr Turnbow was convicted.

(F3) "By the way, what's the big word?" *St. Louis Post-Dispatch*

(F4) In 1964 eleven civil rights campaigners were murdered in Mississippi. It was only after the deaths of John Chaney, Michael Schwerner and Andrew Goodman that the media became interested in the murders of the civil rights workers. Michael Schwerner's widow made a statement to the newspapers on the murders.

My husband did not die in vain. If he and Andrew Goodman had been Negro, the world would have taken little notice of their death. After all the slaying of a Negro in Mississippi is not news. It is only because my husband and Andrew Goodman were white that the national alarm has been sounded.

(F5) In 1963 President Kennedy proposed a Civil Rights Bill. On June 11, 1963 he explained on radio and television why he wanted the country to support this bill. It included a section that would guarantee blacks the right to vote.

The Negro baby born in America today, regardless of the section or the state in which he is born, has about one-half as much chance of completing high school as a white baby; one-third as much chance of becoming a professional man; twice as much chance of becoming unemployed; about one-seventh as much chance of earning $10,000 a year; a life expectancy which is seven years shorter and the prospects of earning only half as much...

We preach freedom around the world, and we mean it. And we cherish our freedom here at home. But are we to say to the world - and much more importantly to each other - that this is the land of the free, except for the Negroes; that we have no second-class citizens, except Negroes; that we have no class or caste system, no ghettos, no master race, except with respect to Negroes.

(F6) Civil rights demonstration in Selma, Alabama.

(F7) In Selma, Alabama, the 15,000 black population meant that blacks were in a majority. However, only 350 of these were registered voters and the town was ruled by white politicians. In January 1965 the Student Nonviolent Coordinating Committee started a campaign to register black voters in Selma. Blacks who queued up to register were arrested. During the campaign Viola Luizzo, Jimmie Jackson and Reverend James Reeb were murdered and 3,800 demonstrators were arrested. After three months only fifty black people had been successfully registered. The Student Nonviolent Coordinating Committee organised a protest march from Selma to Montgomery, the state capital. Sheyann Webb, who was nine-years-old at the time, described several years later what happened.

The troopers could be seen more clearly now. I guess I was fifty to seventy-five yards from them. They were wearing blue helmets, blue jackets, and they carried clubs in their hands... I heard this voice speaking over the bullhorn saying this was an unlawful assembly and for us to disperse and go back to the church... Then I stepped out a way and looked again and saw the troopers putting on their gas masks... Everyone got down on their knees, and I did too, and somebody was saying for us to pray... Then I heard all this screaming and the people were turning and I saw the first part of the line running and stumbling back towards us... somebody yelled, "Oh, God, they're killing us!"... I heard a shout "Gas! Gas!"... I saw those horseman coming toward me and they had those awful masks on; they rode right through the cloud of tear gas. Some of them had clubs, others had ropes or whips, which they swung about them like they were driving cattle... You could hear the horses' hooves on the pavement and you'd hear the whips swishing and you'd hear them striking the people.

(F8) President Johnson, along with millions all over the world, saw these events at Selma on television. Johnson told the nation that he was appalled by the violence he had seen and intended to take action. Later that year, Johnson, the first president from the South to be elected since the Civil War, asked Congress to pass a tough Voting Rights Act.

Every American citizen must have an equal right to vote... Yet the harsh fact is that in many places in this country men and women are kept from voting simply because they are Negroes. Every device of which human ingenuity is capable has been used to deny this right. The Negro citizen may go to register only to be told that the day is wrong, or the hour is late, or the official in charge is absent. And if he persists and he manages to present himself to register, he may be disqualified because he did not spell out his middle name or because he abbreviated a word on the application. And if he manages to fill out an application he is given a test. The registrar is the sole judge of whether he passes his test. He may be asked to recite the entire constitution, or explain the most complex provisions of state laws. And even a college degree cannot be used to prove that he can read and write. For the fact is that the only way to pass these barriers is to show a white skin... This bill will strike down restrictions to voting in all elections - federal, State, and local - which have been used to deny Negroes the right to vote.

(F9) The Voting Rights Act was passed by large majorities in the House of Representatives (333 to 48) and the Senate (77 to 19) and became law in 1965. In 1969 research was carried out to discover if the act had been successful in enabling black people to register.

State	% of white	% of black
Alabama	94.6	61.3
Arkansas	81.6	77.9
Florida	94.2	67.0
Georgia	88.5	60.4
Louisiana	87.1	60.8
Mississippi	89.8	66.5
North Carolina	78.4	53.7
South Carolina	71.5	54.6
Tennessee	92.0	92.1
Texas	61.8	73.1
Virginia	78.7	59.8
Total	80.4	64.8

(F10) Photograph taken during an election
campaign in Tampa, Florida.

(F11) Number of registered black voters in the southern states of Texas, Louisiana, Mississippi, Alabama, Georgia, Florida, South Carolina, North Carolina, Tennessee, Arkansas and Virginia.

1940	250,000
1952	1,008,000
1956	1,238,000
1960	1,463,000
1964	2,164,000
1968	3,112,000
1976	4,000,000
1982	4,600,000

(F12) In 1988 Jessie Jackson came second to Michael Dukakis with 7 million votes (2.6 million of those votes were from whites) in his bid to become the presidential candidate for the Democratic Party. His speech at the Democratic convention on July 20, 1988 included the following passage.

My right and privilege to stand here before you have been won - in my lifetime - by the blood and the sweat of the innocent. Many were lost in the struggle to vote. Jimmy Lee Jackson, a young student gave his life. Viola Luizzo, a white mother from Detroit - brains blown out at point-blank range. Schwerner, Goodman and Chaney - two Jews and a black - found in a common grave, bodies riddled with bullets, in Mississippi. The four darling little girls in the church in Birmingham, Alabama. They died that we have a right to vote... As a testament to the struggles of those who have gone before... tomorrow night my name will go into nomination for the presidency of the United States of America.

Questions

1. Explain what is meant in source F1 by: (i) "white supremacy"; (ii)"suffrage".

2. Why is it unlikely that the speeches in source F1 would have been made by white politicians after 1965?

3. Study the sources in this unit. What methods were used to deny black people the right to vote?

4. How might James Eastland (F1) and Lyndon Johnson (F8) have reacted to source F4?

5. How did the events described in sources F4 and F7 help to achieve the vote for black people in the South.

6. "Sources F5 and F8 are both taken from politician's speeches and are therefore biased and of little value to the historian." Referring to the two sources, show to what extent you agree with this statement.

7. Sources F6 and F7 both deal with police action in Selma on March 21, 1965. Which source is the most effective in communicating what took place on the march?

8. What do you learn from sources F9, F11 and F12 on the success of the 1965 Voting Rights Act?

9. "The 1965 Voting Rights Act was the most important civil rights legislation passed in the United States this century." With reference to the sources in this unit and other material that you have studied, show to what extent you agree with this statement.

Bibliography

William Ames (ed.)	The Negro Struggle for Equality	D. C. Heath	1965
John Ansbro	Martin Luther King	Fowler Wright	1982
H. Aptheker (ed.)	The Negro People in the USA	Citadel	1969
Daisy Bates	The Long Shadow of Little Rock	David McKay	1962
Lerone Bennett	Before the Mayflower	Johnson Publishing	1961
Lerone Bennett	Martin Luther King	Johnson Publishing	1964
Thomas Brooks	Walls Come Tumbling Down	Prentice-Hall	1974
Ames H. Brown	The Negro Struggle for Equality	D. C. Heath	1965
Henry Commager (ed.)	The Struggle for Racial Equality	Harper & Row	1967
Earl Conrad	Jim Crow America	Duell, Sloan & Pearce	1947
James Cook	The Segregationists	Appleton	1962
Theodore Cross	The Black Power Imperative	Faulkner	1987
Mary Ellison	The Black Experience	Batsford	1974
James Farmer	Freedom When?	Random House	1965
Charles Fager	Selma 1965	Beacon	1974
William Foster	Negro People in American History	International Press	1954
John Hope Franklin	From Slavery to Freedom	Alfred Korpf	1956
J. L. Franklin	Journey Toward Hope	University of Oklahoma	1971
Thomas Frazier (ed.)	Afro-American History	Harcourt, Brace & World	1970
David Garrow	The FBI and Martin Luther King	W. W. Norton	1981
Kenneth Goode	From Africa to the United States	Scott & Foreman	1969
Joanne Grant	Black Protest	St. Martins Press	1968
William B. Huie	He Slew the Dreamer	W.H. Allen	1970
Stetson Kennedy	I Rode With the Ku Klux Klan	Arco Publishers	1954
Eric Lincoln	The Black Muslims in America	Beacon	1961
Louis Lomax	The Negro Revolt	Signet	1962
Martin Luther King	Stride Towards Freedom	Harper & Row	1958
Martin Luther King	Why We Can't Wait	Harper & Row	1963
Martin Luther King	The Strength to Love	Harper & Row	1963
Martin Luther King	Where Do We Go From Here?	Harper & Row	1967
J. Washington (ed.)	Writings of Martin Luther King	Harper & Row	1986
John Mecklin	The Ku Klux Klan	Russell & Russell	1963
Milton Meltzer (ed.)	A History of the American Negro	Thomas Crowell	1966
John Bartlow Martin	The Deep South Says Never	Ballantine	1957
Penelope McPhee	King Remembered	W. W. Norton	1986
James Peck	Freedom Ride	Simon & Schuster	1962
William Randel	The Ku Klux Klan	Hamish Hamilton	1965
Stanley Seaberg	The Negro in American History	Scholastic	1968
Arthur Thomas	Like It Is	E. P. Dutton	1981
Melvin Tumin	Desegregation	Princeton	1958
Wyn Craig Wade	The Fiery Cross	Simon & Schuster	1987
Thomas Wagstaff (ed.)	Black Power	Glencoe Press	1969
Ida Wells	Crusade for Justice	University of Chicago	1970
W. J. Wetherby	Breaking the Silence	Penguin	1965
Joel Williamson (ed.)	The Origins of Segregation	D. C. Heath	1968
Allen Weinstein (ed.)	The Segregation Era	Oxford University Press	1970
Malcolm X	Malcolm X Speaks	Secker & Warburg	1965
Malcolm X	The Autobiography of Malcolm X	Hutchinson	1965

Acknowledgments

Sources: (A1) Ho Chi Minh, *La Correspondence Internationale*, 1924; (A3) *Vicksburg Evening Post*, May 4, 1919; (A10) *Sunday Times Magazine*, January 31, 1988; (B1) Ida Wells, *Crusade For Justice*, University of Chicago, 1970; (B5) *Crisis Magazine*, May 1919; (B6) Richard Wright, *12 Million Black Voices*, Paul Reynolds, 1939; (C1) (i) *Christian Century Magazine*, February 1957; (iii) *Ebony Magazine*, July 1959; (iv) *Saturday Review*, April 1965; (v) *Look Magazine*, April 1968; (C3) *New York Times*, May 31, 1963; (C5) James Peck, *Freedom Ride*, Simon & Schuster, 1962; (C6) (ii) speech, Harlem, December 31, 1964; (iii) speech, Militant Labour Forum, January 7, 1965; (C8) Martin Luther King, *Why We Can't Wait*, Harper & Row, 1963; (C9) Arthur Thomas (ed.), *Like It Is*, E.P. Dutton, 1981; (D4) *Ebony Magazine*, October 1966; (D6) Daisey Bates, *The Long Shadow of Little Rock*, David McKay, 1962; (D7) *New York Times*, September 24, 1957; (D9) *New York Times*, September 27, 1957; (D11) *Eyes on the Prize*, Blackside Productions, 1986; (D13) Mary Ellison, *The Black Experience*, Batsford, 1974; (E1) Martin Luther King, *Stride Towards Freedom: The Montgomery Story*, Harper & Row, 1958; (E4) Arthur Thomas (ed.), *Like It Is*, E.P. Dutton, 1981; (E6) James Peck, *Freedom Ride*, Simon & Schuster, 1962; (E9) *Eyes on the Prize*, Blackside Productions, 1986; (E11) James Farmer, *Freedom When?*, Random House, 1965; (G6) Frank Sikora (ed.) *Selma, Lord, Selma: Childhood Memories of the Civil-Rights Days*, University of Alabama, 1980

Picture Credits: Library of Congress: pages 6 and 8; Black Star: page 10; Schomburg Collection: pages 12, 14(r) and 19; Tuskegee Institute: pages 14(l) and 21; United Press: pages 23, 27, 30, 50, 53, 61, 62, and 67; Flip Schulke: pages 25 and 51; Wide World: pages 32, 35, 65 and 75; New York Museum of Modern Art: page 39; Magnum: page 44; Southern Patriot: pages 47 and 57; Topham: page 58; Congress of Racial Equality: page 68; St Louis Post-Dispatch: page 71; Poppofoto: page 72.